S0-BBR-042

?WHAT IF...

SHARKS

Steve Parker

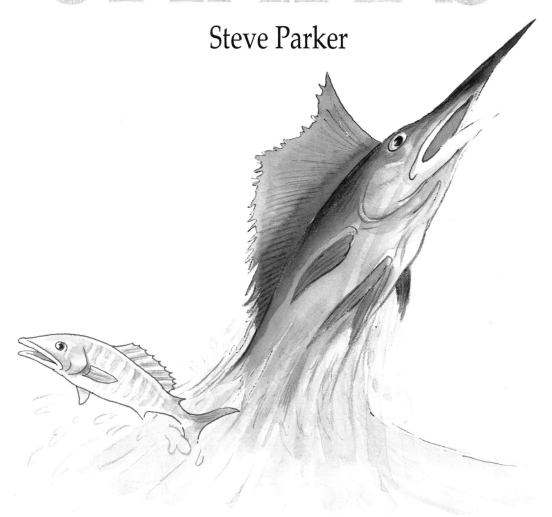

Copper Beech Books
Brookfield, Connecticut

7466410

CONTENTS

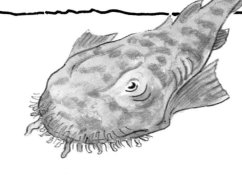

© Aladdin Books Ltd 1996
Designed and produced by
Aladdin Books Ltd
28 Percy Street
London W1P 0LD

First Published in the United States
in 1996 by
Copper Beech Books, an imprint of
The Millbrook Press
2 Old New Milford Road
Brookfield, Connecticut 06804

Editor
Jon Richards

Designed by
David West Children's Books
Designers
Rob Shone and Ed Simkins

Illustrator
Tony Kenyon – B. L. Kearley Ltd

Printed in Belgium
All rights reserved

Library of Congress Cataloging-in-
Publication Data
Parker, Steve.
Sharks / by Steve Parker : illustrated by
Tony Kenyon. p. cm. — (What if—)
Includes index. Summary: Examines the
world of fishes—from terrifying sharks to
graceful sea horses—using a series of
questions such as "What if a lungfish
crawled out of the water?" and "What if a
coral didn't build reefs?"
ISBN 0-7613-0456-8 (lib. bdg.). —
ISBN 0-7613-0471-1 (pbk.) 1. Marine
fishes—Miscellanea—Juvenile literature.
[1. Fishes—Miscellanea. 2. Questions and
answers.] I. Kenyon, Tony, ill. II. Title. III.
Series: Parker, Steve. What if—
QL620.P38 1996   95-50311
507'.31—dc20   CIP AC

WHAT IF THERE WERE NO INTRODUCTION?

Well, you wouldn't be reading this! The *What if...?* books look at the world around us from a very unusual angle. Instead of merely explaining the world around us as we know it, they make it exciting and much more interesting by asking *What if...* things were very different?

Nearly seven-tenths of the Earth is covered by water. This wet world has provided a superb environment for one of the most diverse group of animals – fish. Over 20,000 species of fish have been found so far. But this number is continuously increasing as more and more of these creatures are discovered by scientists probing the deepest recesses of this planet. These wonderful animals range in size from the minute dwarf goby, to the enormous whale shark. They have developed a bizarre collection of features, from the poisonous spines of the lionfish, to the electric organs of the catfish. Who knows what other fascinating shapes are waiting to be discovered in the depths of the world's oceans?

What if Sharks...? takes a look at this underwater realm of fish, describing how these creatures live beneath the waves. It does this in a way that's easy to read and remember, by asking what might happen if... things were different!

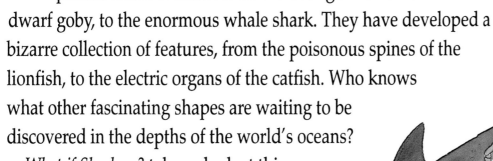

WHAT IF SHARKS WERE THE ONLY FISH?

Sharks form the pinnacle of an enormous food chain that exists in the world's oceans. This includes a whole host of creatures, from the smallest plankton and coral polyps to the largest fish and mammals. These incredibly diverse animals are dependent upon each other for survival. If sharks were the only fish, then there would be nothing for them to eat. They would very quickly starve and die out.

Food chain

Life in the oceans provides an endless cycle of nutrients, beginning with the tiniest, microscopic creatures. These are eaten by larger plankton, shrimp, and small fish, which in turn are eaten by larger fish, such as fry and herring. Finally, we reach the great predators, such as sharks.

When sharks die, their bodies provide food for the microscopic life. So the cycle of nutrients begins again.

What if sharks didn't have teeth?

Most sharks usually have a bristling array of very sharp teeth, set in a jaw that can be chomped together by extremely powerful muscles. These teeth are continuously replaced when they have become blunt. As the old ones fall out, new, sharper teeth that were growing behind take their place.

However, the biggest sharks, the whale shark and the basking shark, have almost no teeth at all. Instead their teeth are extremely small, and in order to eat they have to strain shrimp or plankton from the water.

Tuna

Small fry and shrimp

Plankton

Herring

Aquatic zoo

Many fish have been named after other animals because they share certain characteristics. For example, the catfish has long whiskers which it uses to feel around for food. Sea horses are unlike any other fish. They swim in an upright position with their heads bowed – like a prancing horse. The lionfish has a large mane of spines, which are tipped with a powerful poison. However, the dogfish doesn't look much like its land-living canine counterpart!

Crayfish

When is a fish not a fish?

Just as many fish have been named after other animals, so many animals have been called fish! For example, starfish belong to a group of animals called *echinoderms*, which includes sea cucumbers. Crayfish are, in fact, crustaceans, relatives of lobsters and crabs. Cuttlefish are mollusks and are similar to octopus and squid.

Some sea animals have evolved to look very similar to fish, such as whales and dolphins. These have developed the same sleek body shape as fish, but they are mammals.

Starfish

Cuttlefish

5

WHAT IF A HERRING DIDN'T HAVE SCALES?

A fish without scales would have much less protection against the teeth and spines of predators and enemies. It would be attacked by pests, such as fish lice and other blood-sucking parasites. It could be rubbed and cut by stones or sharp-leafed water plants. The scales of a fish act as a protective coat of armor against the outside world. Most scales are arranged like the shingles of a roof. One edge of the scale, the stalk, is attached to the skin, while the rest of the scale lies flat against the one beneath.

Some fish, like eels, have scales that are hidden by a thick, tough, slimy skin which lies on top of the scales.

Smooth customer
Fish scales are usually arranged with the stalk pointing toward the front. This lets the fish slip through the water.

Flow of water

Tough as old boots

Sharks are covered in special scales called denticles. These are tiny hooks, or teeth, that are embedded in the skin and point backward, making shark's skin extremely abrasive (rough).

They also make the skin extremely hard-wearing. So much so that jackets, vests, belts and even shoes can be made from this tough and highly durable skin.

What if a fish had no skeleton?

Fish can be split into two different groups. Those that have a skeleton made from bone, known as bony fish, and those whose skeleton is made from gristle, or cartilage, known as cartilaginous fish. Even though skeletons vary (right), they are all based on the long spinal column in the middle of the body. This is made of linked parts called vertebrae. From this ribs grow, and at the front is the skull.

The skeleton forms the fish's inner framework, upon which all of its internal organs, skin, and muscles sit. Without it, a fish would be a blob of soft tissue.

Skull

Ribs

Fin rays

Spinal column

No-bone fish

Not all fish have a skeleton made out of bone. Sharks, skates, rays, and chimaeras (e.g. ratfishes) have a skeleton made of cartilage or gristle (left). It's very strong and tough, like bone, but more flexible. These fish are called *cartilaginous fish* or chondrichthyes, and there are about 720 kinds or species.

How can you tell the age of a fish?

Most fish keep growing through life, so the biggest fish of a species are the oldest. Some types of fish, such as salmon, have scales with tiny dark lines on them. These are growth rings. Like the growth rings in a tree trunk, they tell you not only the age of a fish, but also how it has grown through its life. A group of dark lines close together shows the slow growth of one winter. A group of lines that are farther apart indicates faster growth during the summer months.

WHAT IF FISH COULD FLY?

Most fish move by swimming through the water, either by wiggling their body from side to side, or by waving their fins. A few have learned how to use their fins to walk on land (see page 11). Other fish have developed the ability to leap from the water and swoop and glide above the surface for several feet, before plunging back down into the waves. They are called flying fish.

Take off
If they are threatened by a predator, such as a shark, flying fish will gather speed, up to 20 mph (32 km/h), and shoot above the waves.

What if you could ride a sea horse?

Sea horses are true fish, cousins of pipefish and sticklebacks, but with a very strange body shape. The face resembles a horse's head, with small pectoral fins sticking from the neck, one dorsal fin on the back of the stiff body, and a curly tail to wrap around plants or rocks to hold the fish in place. Instead of getting forward movement by swishing its tail, the sea horse waves its dorsal fin very quickly to move itself forward. By swimming at a modest speed, the sea horse can suck or snap any food into its small, tube-shaped mouth.

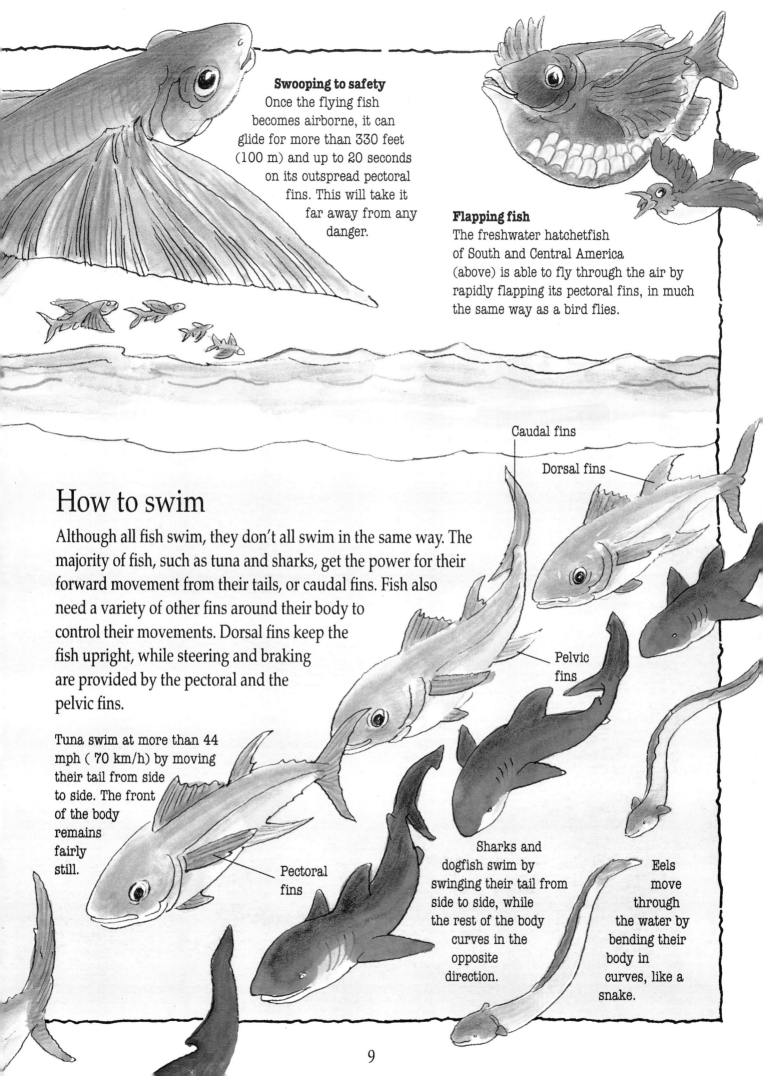

Swooping to safety
Once the flying fish becomes airborne, it can glide for more than 330 feet (100 m) and up to 20 seconds on its outspread pectoral fins. This will take it far away from any danger.

Flapping fish
The freshwater hatchetfish of South and Central America (above) is able to fly through the air by rapidly flapping its pectoral fins, in much the same way as a bird flies.

How to swim

Although all fish swim, they don't all swim in the same way. The majority of fish, such as tuna and sharks, get the power for their forward movement from their tails, or caudal fins. Fish also need a variety of other fins around their body to control their movements. Dorsal fins keep the fish upright, while steering and braking are provided by the pectoral and the pelvic fins.

Tuna swim at more than 44 mph (70 km/h) by moving their tail from side to side. The front of the body remains fairly still.

Caudal fins

Dorsal fins

Pelvic fins

Pectoral fins

Sharks and dogfish swim by swinging their tail from side to side, while the rest of the body curves in the opposite direction.

Eels move through the water by bending their body in curves, like a snake.

9

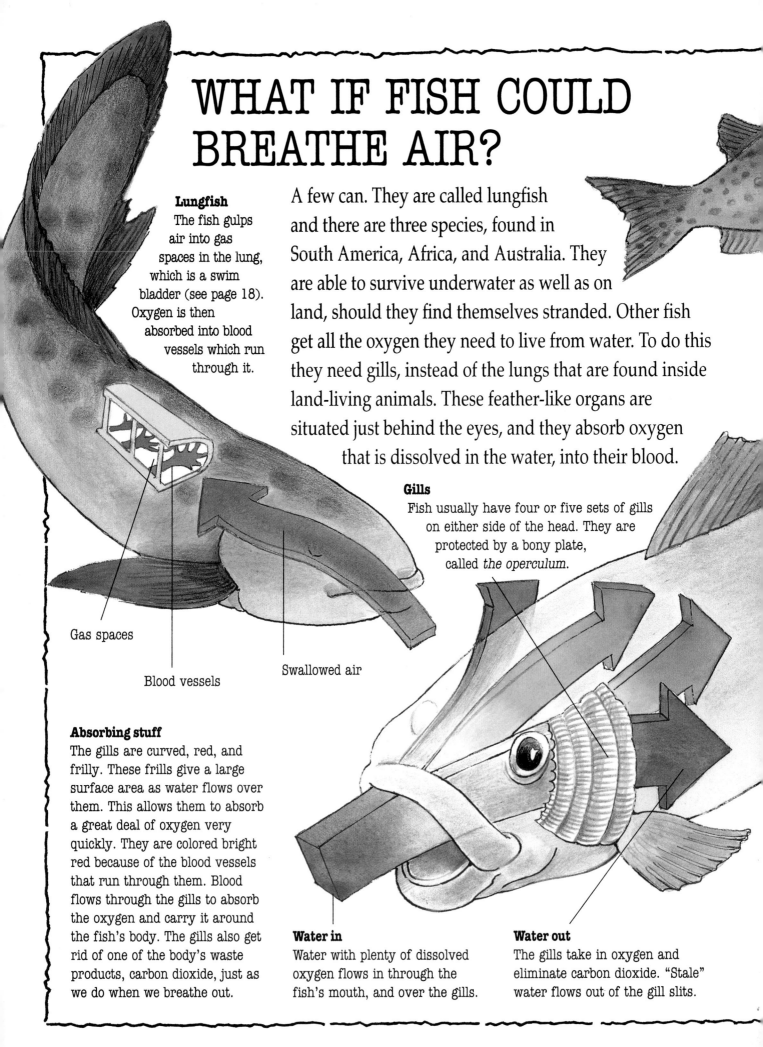

WHAT IF FISH COULD BREATHE AIR?

A few can. They are called lungfish and there are three species, found in South America, Africa, and Australia. They are able to survive underwater as well as on land, should they find themselves stranded. Other fish get all the oxygen they need to live from water. To do this they need gills, instead of the lungs that are found inside land-living animals. These feather-like organs are situated just behind the eyes, and they absorb oxygen that is dissolved in the water, into their blood.

Lungfish
The fish gulps air into gas spaces in the lung, which is a swim bladder (see page 18). Oxygen is then absorbed into blood vessels which run through it.

Gas spaces

Blood vessels

Swallowed air

Gills
Fish usually have four or five sets of gills on either side of the head. They are protected by a bony plate, called *the operculum*.

Absorbing stuff
The gills are curved, red, and frilly. These frills give a large surface area as water flows over them. This allows them to absorb a great deal of oxygen very quickly. They are colored bright red because of the blood vessels that run through them. Blood flows through the gills to absorb the oxygen and carry it around the fish's body. The gills also get rid of one of the body's waste products, carbon dioxide, just as we do when we breathe out.

Water in
Water with plenty of dissolved oxygen flows in through the fish's mouth, and over the gills.

Water out
The gills take in oxygen and eliminate carbon dioxide. "Stale" water flows out of the gill slits.

Catfish
These whiskered fish, such as the upside down catfish, will travel over land, in order to get from one pond to another.

A fish out of water

Several kinds of fish can survive out of water for a short time, and even move across land. They are usually fish that live in tropical swamps, such as catfish, where the pools disappear in the dry season.

The water in these pools is warm and stagnant, with little dissolved oxygen. So the catfish gulps air into pockets in the sides of the gill chambers. Oxygen goes from the air bubbles, through the watery covering of the gills, and into the blood. The gills must always be kept moist. If they dry out, the fish suffocates and dies.

Eels
The eel wriggles through grass and plants, taking in extra oxygen through its moist, slimy, almost scaleless skin.

Mudskippers
The mudskipper lives along muddy tropical shores. It has very large gill chambers and refreshes the water in these every few minutes. It can walk on its armlike pectoral fins or surf across mud with its tail.

Bubble and squeak

Although they can't scream and shout, many fish can make noises. They do this by squeezing air bubbles that they have swallowed through their swim bladder, in just the same way as your stomach rumbles from time to time.

They can also make noises by rubbing together bones or fin spines.

The sounds may be to frighten enemies, attract mates, or keep in touch with neighbors. Some of these noisy fish are named after the sound they produce, such as drumfish, squeaker catfish, grunter gurnards, snorter horsemackerels, and singing midshipmen.

WHAT IF A LANTERN FISH COULDN'T SEE?

Sight is only one of the impressive array of senses that fish use to detect the underwater world, and is only really useful in the bright, sunlit surface waters. Fish from the dim and murky midwater, between 660 and 3,300 feet (200 and 1,000 m) deep, such as the lantern fish, may have even larger eyes, to let in as much light as possible. To survive in these darker waters, as well as in the completely black depths, fish must employ their other senses to detect the world around them. Some deepsea and cavefish are totally blind and so rely entirely on their other senses. These senses include smell to scent blood in the water, touch to detect changes in currents or approaching fish, and even detection by using electrical currents.

Lens

Cornea

Retina

Lateral line

Fish eyes
Light enters the fish's eye through the transparent domed cornea. It is then bent or focused by a very thick lens, and shines onto the retina. This turns the picture into nerve signals and sends these along a nerve to the brain.

How do fish feel?

Fish can feel in the same way as humans, by detecting any direct touches on their body and fins.

They can also feel currents, swirls, and vibrations coming through the water. These are detected by the silvery stripe that runs along each side of the fish's body, called the *lateral line*. These are incredibly sensitive, and tell the fish about any underwater sounds and movements, and about the position of nearby objects. The fish can use them to sense predators or prey, and avoid bumping into rocks, even in the total darkness of the deep sea.

A shocking experience

Some fish use shocks of electricity to find their way, repel enemies, or stun victims (see page 15). These include the elephant-snout fish, the knifefish and torpedo-rays.

The elephant-snout fish uses electricity as a means of sensing. It makes a weak electrical field around itself by sending out pulses of electricity from its special organs. Its nose and tail detect the field, which is bent or altered by the presence of nearby creatures, rocks, and other objects. They can also detect the tiny electric charges made by another animal's muscles as it moves nearby. The elephant-snout fish grubs in the mud on the bottom and finds food such as water snails and worms, even in cloudy water.

Smelling something fishy!

Sharks use scent to detect their prey. They can "smell" certain substances in the water, even in very tiny quantities. A shark can detect the smallest drop of blood and, thinking it may be a wounded animal, may swim over looking for a meal!

Other fish use their noses to sniff out their food, as well as to recognize other fish of the same species. They are also able to tell the difference between water plants, and even the waters from different streams.

WHAT IF AN ANGLER WENT FISHING?

Fish have developed an array of different adaptations. These range from poisonous spines to inflatable bodies! They can be used either to catch something to eat, or to stop the fish from being eaten.

Anglerfish are a family of fish with a long, fleshy pole (barbel) growing from their forehead. The barbel can be colored, or even illuminated. The anglerfish goes fishing with this barbel to lure unwary prey.

Living seaweed

The leafy sea horse looks as much like a piece of seaweed as a fish. Its body is covered in leaf-like growths. When this sea horse lies still in seaweed, it is virtually impossible to spot, allowing it to hide from any predators.

Swimming plants

Many fish are masters of camouflage, hiding themselves from their prey or predators. Some have developed to look like plants. For example, pipefish (see page 17) are very thin and hang among the leaves of eelgrass, making themselves almost invisible. Those fish that cannot hide themselves have to use speed and agility to escape from being somebody's lunch.

Wobbegong

The frill around the jaw of this shark ensures that it remains hidden from its prey until the last moment. It lurks on the seabed, waiting for a scrap of food to come along.

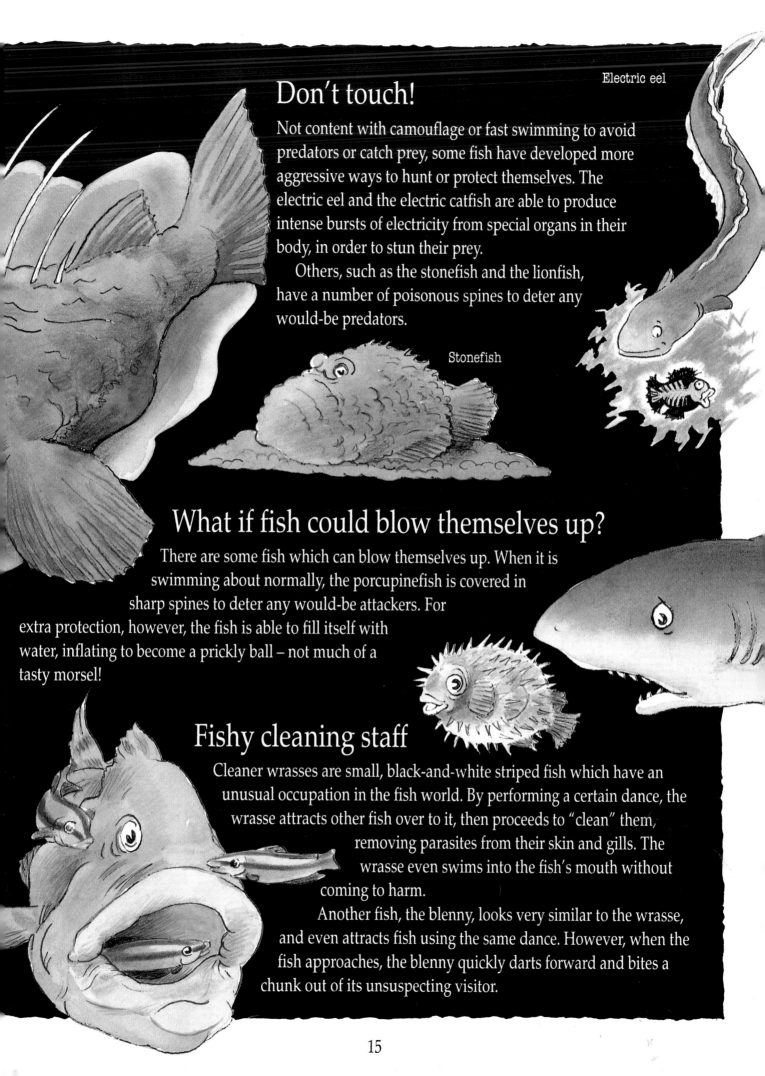

Don't touch!

Not content with camouflage or fast swimming to avoid predators or catch prey, some fish have developed more aggressive ways to hunt or protect themselves. The electric eel and the electric catfish are able to produce intense bursts of electricity from special organs in their body, in order to stun their prey.

Others, such as the stonefish and the lionfish, have a number of poisonous spines to deter any would-be predators.

Stonefish

What if fish could blow themselves up?

There are some fish which can blow themselves up. When it is swimming about normally, the porcupinefish is covered in sharp spines to deter any would-be attackers. For extra protection, however, the fish is able to fill itself with water, inflating to become a prickly ball – not much of a tasty morsel!

Fishy cleaning staff

Cleaner wrasses are small, black-and-white striped fish which have an unusual occupation in the fish world. By performing a certain dance, the wrasse attracts other fish over to it, then proceeds to "clean" them, removing parasites from their skin and gills. The wrasse even swims into the fish's mouth without coming to harm.

Another fish, the blenny, looks very similar to the wrasse, and even attracts fish using the same dance. However, when the fish approaches, the blenny quickly darts forward and bites a chunk out of its unsuspecting visitor.

WHAT IF SALMON COULDN'T MIGRATE?

Every year, salmon swim vast distances from the sea, up the same rivers they hatched, to reproduce. If they could not migrate, then they could not lay their eggs in the fresh water, and they would soon die out.

Fish have many bizarre ways of reproducing. Some may give birth to live young instead of laying eggs, while with others it is the male that gets pregnant!

One on one

In the vast ocean depths, you might not meet another living thing for days. Finding a mate is difficult. If a male deep-sea anglerfish meets a female, they take no chances and hang on to each other. The male grows into the body of the female and stays stuck to her. He lives off her blood and body fluids, like a parasite. When she is ready to lay her eggs, he is right there to fertilize them with his sperm.

Spawning
Exhausted after the journey, the female and male salmon spawn. She lays eggs and he sheds sperm to fertilize them.

Growing up
In spring, the eggs hatch into babies, called *alevins*. They grow into fry, then parr.

Little love nest

The male stickleback builds a nest from debris he has found on the river bottom. He will then try to lure a female to lay her eggs inside. The male will then deposit his sperm on the eggs to fertilize them.

The long swim home

The full-grown salmon swims back against the current of the stream in which it was born. It will probably have to negotiate many obstacles, including canal locks and waterfalls.

What if males had babies?

The males of some fish, such as sea horses and pipefish, gather eggs, which have been laid by the female and look after them while they develop. The male keeps the eggs protected in a pocketlike part on his body made of flaps of skin, called the *brood pouch*. When the babies hatch, they swim out of the pouch opening.

Staying at sea

Salmon may live at sea for up to five years. During this time, they grow large and sleek.

Open wide

Some cichlid fish have a peculiar way of looking after their offspring. They care for both the eggs and babies in their mouth. They are known as mouth-brooders.

When the baby cichlids have hatched, they swim in a cloud around their parent. When danger appears, the cloud of babies swims straight back into the safety of the parent's mouth.

Leaving home

After four years, the parr turn silvery and become smolts. They head downriver, and out to sea.

A live birth

Most fish lay eggs, from which their young hatch. This includes sharks, whose eggs are large and in leathery cases with trailing tendrils. Empty egg cases of sharks, skates, and rays are sometimes washed up on the beach as "mermaids' purses." Other sharks, such as the white-tip shark, have eggs that hatch inside the mother, and the young emerge from the reproductive opening, called the *cloaca*.

WHAT IF SHARKS STOPPED SWIMMING?

They would sink to the bottom and stay there. Most fish have an inner body part like an adjustable gas bag, called a swim bladder. The fish adjusts the amount of gas in the bladder to float up or down. Sharks and other cartilaginous fish lack swim bladders and can only stay up by swimming, using their rigid fins like a plane's wings.

Sharks cannot pump water over their gills, like other fish. They need to swim to get oxygen from the water into their blood. If they were to stop they would need a current of water to stay alive.

Stomach

Gills

Brain

Mouth

Heart

Liver

Which fish have wings but cannot fly?

Rays and skates are flattened cartilaginous fish. Their bodies have developed into a squashed, wing-shaped form. This is perfect for their bottom-dwelling lifestyle, where they scavenge or eat seabed creatures. While skates have a tail they can use to swim like other fish, a ray cannot swish its body from side to side, so it flaps its wings up and down to "fly" through the water.

The largest ray is the Pacific manta or devilfish. It has a "wingspan" of more than 20 feet (6 m) – about the same as a hang-glider – and weighs almost two tons. Stingrays have a sharp spine sticking out of the tail, which they can jab into enemies to inject terrible stinging poison.

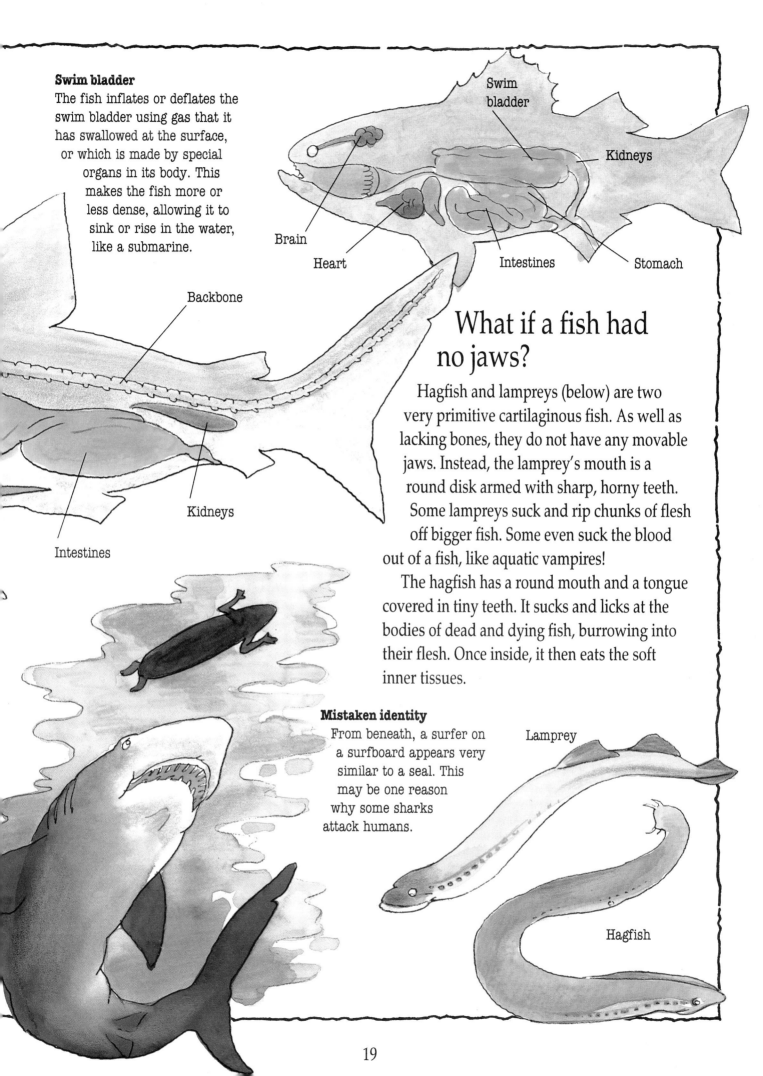

Swim bladder

The fish inflates or deflates the swim bladder using gas that it has swallowed at the surface, or which is made by special organs in its body. This makes the fish more or less dense, allowing it to sink or rise in the water, like a submarine.

Swim bladder

Kidneys

Brain

Heart

Intestines

Stomach

Backbone

Kidneys

Intestines

What if a fish had no jaws?

Hagfish and lampreys (below) are two very primitive cartilaginous fish. As well as lacking bones, they do not have any movable jaws. Instead, the lamprey's mouth is a round disk armed with sharp, horny teeth. Some lampreys suck and rip chunks of flesh off bigger fish. Some even suck the blood out of a fish, like aquatic vampires!

The hagfish has a round mouth and a tongue covered in tiny teeth. It sucks and licks at the bodies of dead and dying fish, burrowing into their flesh. Once inside, it then eats the soft inner tissues.

Mistaken identity

From beneath, a surfer on a surfboard appears very similar to a seal. This may be one reason why some sharks attack humans.

Lamprey

Hagfish

The saltwater fish is hardy enough to stand the high salt content found in sea water conditions. But if it were placed in fresh water it would lose control of its body fluids and absorb too much water.

WHAT IF A SEAFISH SWAM IN FRESH WATER?

Altogether, there are about 8,500 species of freshwater fish that swim in the many streams, rivers, and lakes throughout the world. These include the trout, the perch, and the fearsome pike.

Freshwater fish and seafish have developed bodies to cope with their own environments. There are very few fish that can live in both. If a seafish tried to swim in fresh water, it would blow up like a balloon.

Shriveled fish
A freshwater fish placed in saltwater would shrivel up. Even though it would be surrounded by water, a freshwater fish would find the sea too salty and could not control the water balance of its own body. It would rapidly lose its body fluids and die.

Giants of the rivers

The size of some freshwater fish is only governed by the availability of food and the space they are given to live in. With a lot to eat and roam in, some fish have grown to giant proportions. The arapaima of the Amazon river can reach a length of nearly 10 feet (3 m), and there are stories of it eating small children! Other river giants include the pla beuk which swims in the water of the Mekong river in China. It can grow over 10 feet (3 m), and weighs more than 530 lbs (240 kg) – that's over three times the weight of an adult human! At the other end of the scale is the Chagos dwarf goby, which is only 0.3 inches (8 mm) long.

What if fish could live in seas and rivers?

A few fish found in fresh water are able to survive in the salty sea. Salmon feed and grow in the ocean before swimming up the same river in which they were born, in order to spawn.

Common eels are actually born in the middle of the ocean. They then spend a couple of years drifting on the ocean currents, before swimming up rivers to feed and grow into adults, and then return to the sea.

Sturgeon

Salmon

Eel

Brown trout

Stealth-hunter

Pike are vicious hunters found in most northern lakes and rivers. Their slender bodies make them particularly speedy through tranquil waters. The larger pikes feed on fish, birds, and even mammals!

Hunters of rivers and lakes

As with sharks in the sea, freshwater habitats have their own hunters. In fact, there are cases in which sharks have swam into river estuaries to feed on the fish there!

Thresher sharks are renowned for this, and have even attacked people who thought they were safe in the freshwater estuaries of rivers.

Other fishy hunters, like piranha, swarm together in large, powerful schools, looking for something to eat. If they come across a fish or other animal that shows signs of being wounded or in trouble, these fish will attack, and eat the creatures in a matter of seconds.

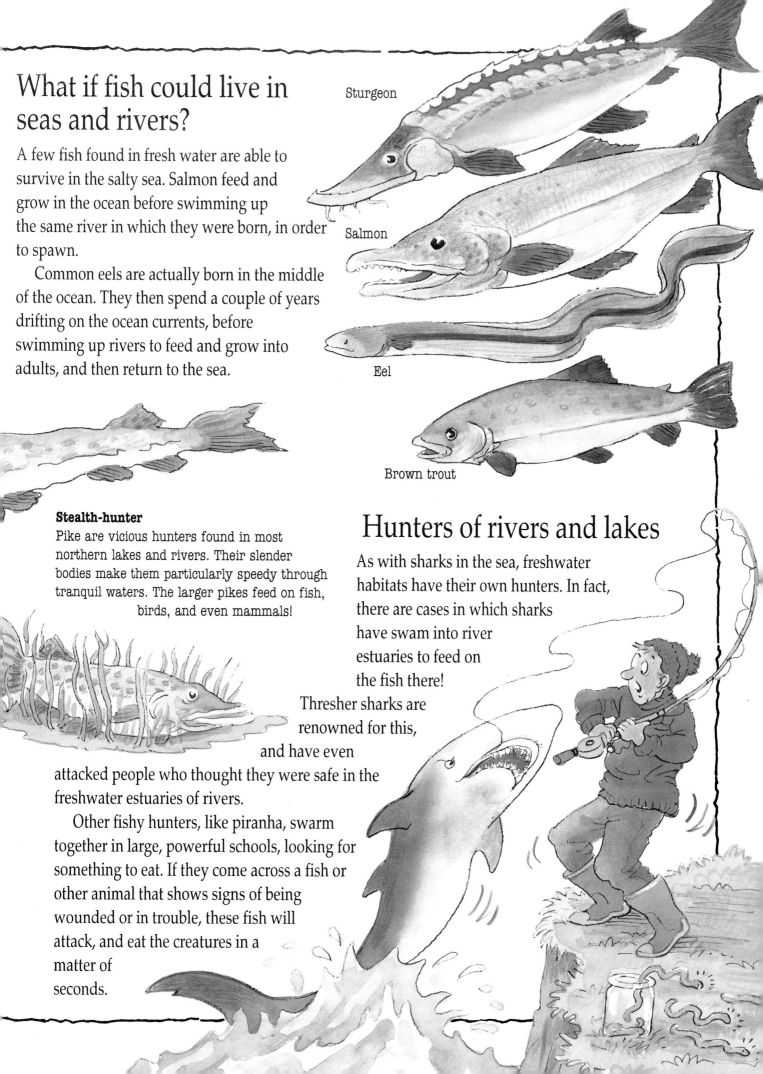

WHAT IF CORAL DIDN'T BUILD REEFS?

We wouldn't have some of the richest and most colorful wildlife habitats on the planet, and the many fish that populate the reefs would be left without a home. Reefs are massive natural structures that are built by tiny animals, called coral polyps. The Great Barrier Reef, off the coast of Australia, stretches over 2,000 km (1,250 miles).

The reef forms only one of many coastal environments, which can also include mudflats, sandbanks, rocky shores, and beaches. The shallow waters are packed full of food, such as seaweeds and invertebrate (backbone-less) animals that a huge diversity of fish, from clownfish to sharks, can feed on.

Biodiversity
A patch of seashore in North America or Europe might have 50 different fish species. A same-sized patch of tropical coral reef could have 500, as well as other animals, from anemones to starfish.

What if a fish had a beak?

The parrotfish found swimming around many coral reefs is so called because it has a hard, horny mouth, rather like the beak of a parrot. This has been formed by the fish's teeth that have fused together.

The parrotfish uses its hard mouth to scrape at the stony skeletons that the coral have left behind. It does not feed on the rock itself, but on the tiny coral animals and other small creatures. As the fish clears a patch and moves on, new coral polyps and other creatures settle on the exposed rock. The whole process usually balances out, so while the fish is feeding itself, the coral polyps continue to build the reef.

Shedding light

Coastal waters have such an incredible wealth of creatures because of the sunlight that can reach the seabed. Here, plants and coral convert this large amount of sunlight into energy, to grow. With this rich basis of plants and simple animals, such as plankton, coastal waters teem with fish and other animals.

Hiding places

The many nooks and crannies scattered throughout the coral reef offer excellent hiding places for both hunters and hunted.

Fishy sleeping bag

During the night, day-active (diurnal) fish settle and rest in the reef. One type of parrotfish even makes a covering of mucus around itself, like a slimy sleeping bag. This traps a layer of water around this fish, and protects it should the fish be attacked, or exposed by the retreating tide.

Meanwhile, as darkness falls, night-active (nocturnal) fish and other animals, such as sea urchins and starfish, come out to feed.

Predators

Sharks, barracuda, and other large fish cruise the reef, looking for a victim that is old, injured, sick, or off guard.

Disappearing grass

Garden eels and sand eels live in tube-shaped burrows on the seabed. As they poke out the front part of the body to catch food floating past, they look like a patch of waving grass. Should danger loom, the eels quickly whisk down into their burrows. In less than a second, the lawn of eels has disappeared into the sandy sea floor.

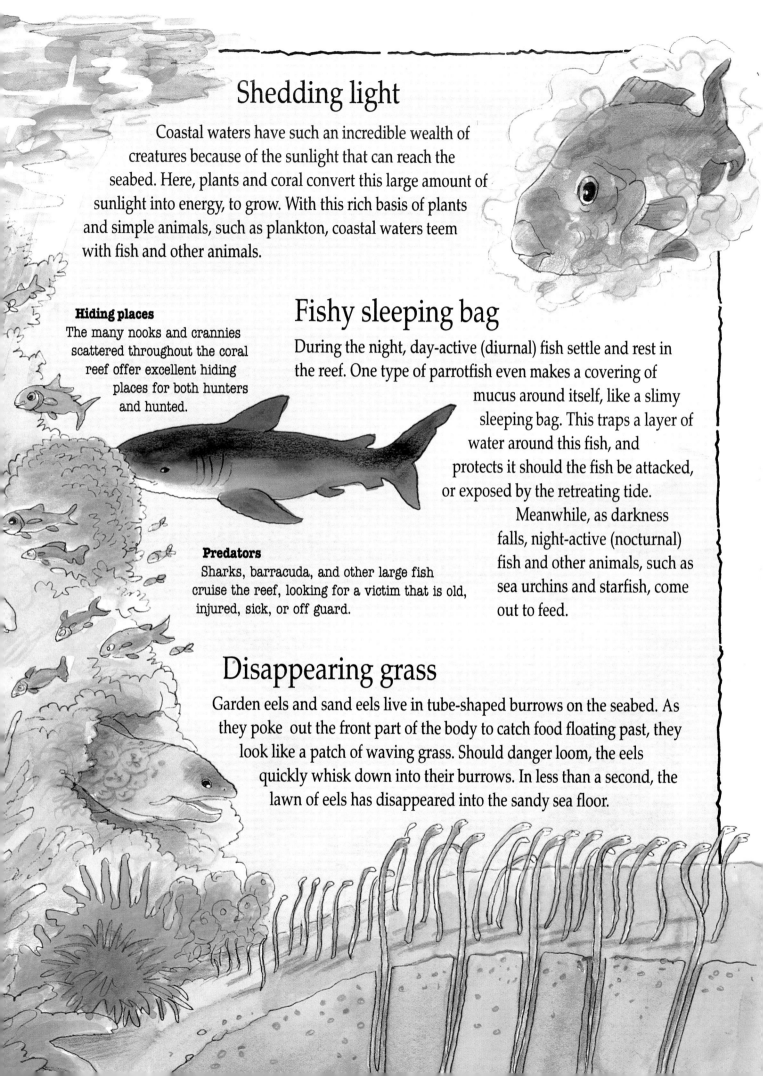

WHAT IF FISH DIDN'T SWIM IN SCHOOLS?

They might easily be caught and eaten by one of the ocean's many hunters! Some species of fish, particularly those found in the open ocean, such as cod and herring, form themselves into enormous groups called *shoals*, or schools. These schools can have as few as 25 individuals, or as many as several thousand fish, all of them swimming in the same direction. These schools have nothing to do with education. Instead, the dense collections of fish protect themselves by dazzling the hunter with a silvery blur. Other open-water fish have developed weapons or incredible speed to avoid predators or catch their prey.

Open ocean sword-fighter

The swordfish has a long, sharp, pointed nose, much like a sword. It uses this to defend itself, and also to stun and kill its prey with slashing strokes. The sharp nose also helps to make the fish extremely streamlined, allowing it to slice through the water at very high speeds.

Underwater pilots

The pilotfish swims very near other large sea animals, such as sharks, giving the impression that it is guiding the bigger creature. This is not the case. Instead, this small, striped fish merely follows the creature around the water. It can feed on any scraps of food that the shark leaves after it has made a kill. Pilotfish are extremely agile and so can easily dodge a lumbering shark if it tries to eat them.

What is the fastest fish?

The fastest fish in the world live in the oceans, far from shore. They need their speed either to dodge predators or catch prey. Over short distances the sailfish is the quickest thing in the water. In short bursts, it can swim at an amazing speed of nearly 70 mph (110 km/h). To achieve this, its body needs to be extremely streamlined, otherwise the turbulence it creates in the water would slow it down. The streamlining is further enhanced by its almost scaleless skin. In parts of the body where there are scales, they are set well below the skin's surface to prevent them causing turbulence. Other very fast fish include the wahoo and the blue-fin tuna. These can swim at more than 40 mph (65 km/h).

Wahoo

Sailfish

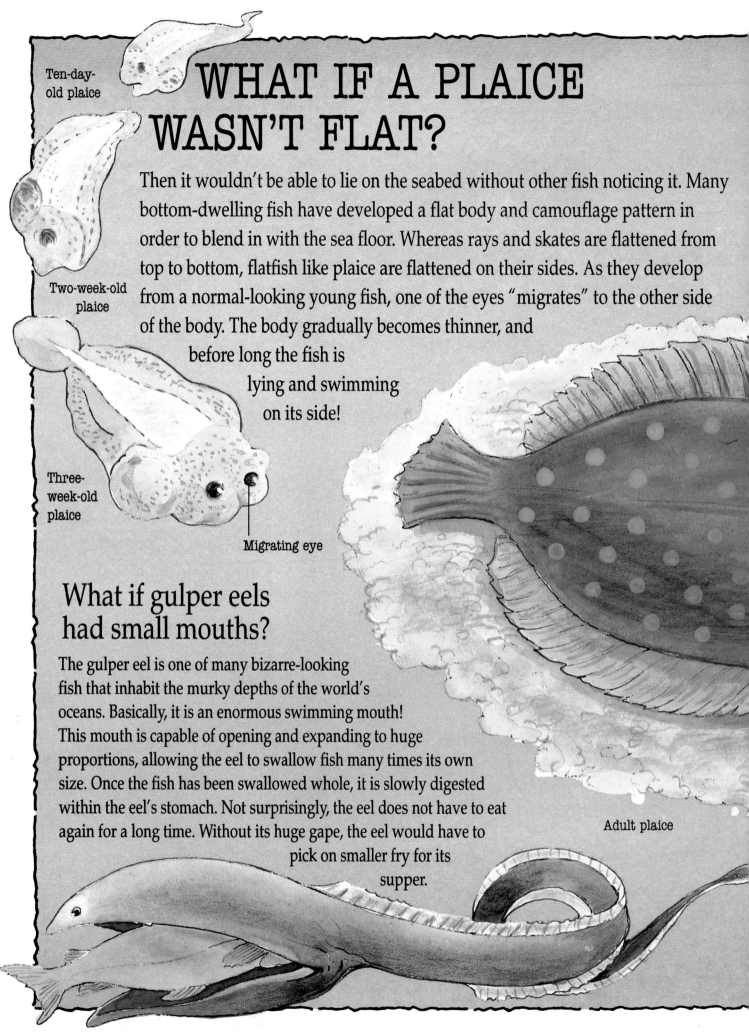

Ten-day-old plaice

Two-week-old plaice

WHAT IF A PLAICE WASN'T FLAT?

Then it wouldn't be able to lie on the seabed without other fish noticing it. Many bottom-dwelling fish have developed a flat body and camouflage pattern in order to blend in with the sea floor. Whereas rays and skates are flattened from top to bottom, flatfish like plaice are flattened on their sides. As they develop from a normal-looking young fish, one of the eyes "migrates" to the other side of the body. The body gradually becomes thinner, and before long the fish is lying and swimming on its side!

Three-week-old plaice

Migrating eye

What if gulper eels had small mouths?

The gulper eel is one of many bizarre-looking fish that inhabit the murky depths of the world's oceans. Basically, it is an enormous swimming mouth! This mouth is capable of opening and expanding to huge proportions, allowing the eel to swallow fish many times its own size. Once the fish has been swallowed whole, it is slowly digested within the eel's stomach. Not surprisingly, the eel does not have to eat again for a long time. Without its huge gape, the eel would have to pick on smaller fry for its supper.

Adult plaice

26

Fish on stilts

The tripod fish gets its name from the three highly developed fins that hang beneath its body. When the tripod fish isn't swimming through the dark deep ocean, it rests on the seabed. It uses its elongated fins like a set of stilts, keeping its body above the slimy ooze and mud that coat the sea floor.

Once on the seabed, the tripod fish can "walk" along the bottom, as it waits for any morsels of food to come along. Other fish that rest and "walk" on their fins are lizardfish and some types of gurnards.

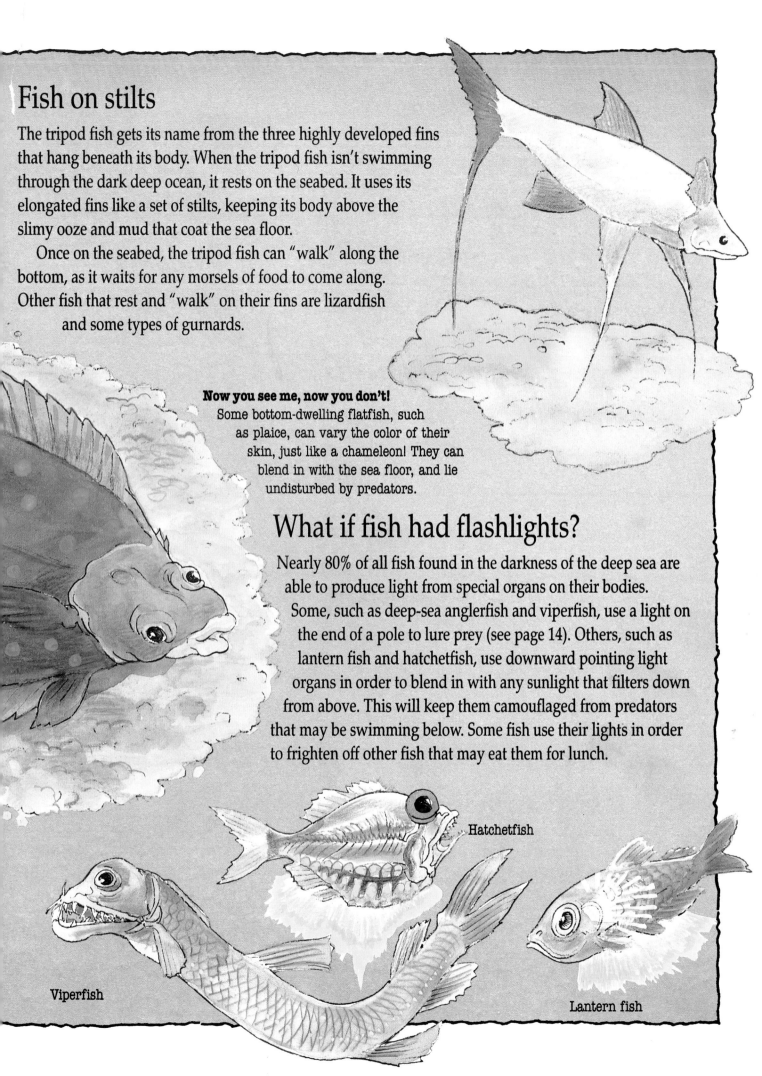

Now you see me, now you don't!
Some bottom-dwelling flatfish, such as plaice, can vary the color of their skin, just like a chameleon! They can blend in with the sea floor, and lie undisturbed by predators.

What if fish had flashlights?

Nearly 80% of all fish found in the darkness of the deep sea are able to produce light from special organs on their bodies.

Some, such as deep-sea anglerfish and viperfish, use a light on the end of a pole to lure prey (see page 14). Others, such as lantern fish and hatchetfish, use downward pointing light organs in order to blend in with any sunlight that filters down from above. This will keep them camouflaged from predators that may be swimming below. Some fish use their lights in order to frighten off other fish that may eat them for lunch.

Hatchetfish

Viperfish

Lantern fish

WHAT IF THERE WERE NO MORE FISH?

In some lakes and rivers, and in some parts of the oceans, there are hardly any fish left. They have all been caught in nets or on lines, as food for people, pets, and farm animals; or they have been hooked by anglers for sport; or the water is so dirty and polluted that fish and other creatures cannot survive.

Many animals and plants rely on fish, whether it is the meat of their bodies or the nutrients from their decaying corpses. Either way, fish form a vital part of the watery ecosystem. If they were to disappear, as may happen in some parts of the world, the effects on the environment could be disastrous – many other species of animal could die out, too.

Global trash bin

Every day we humans dump thousands of tons of garbage, waste, and chemicals into the streams, rivers, and oceans of the world. But we hardly ever see the damage this causes.

We might notice an otter or a seabird on the surface, covered with oil from a ship that has illegally washed out its tanks. But we don't notice the thousands of fish suffocating and dying below the surface. The animal and plant life in many rivers and parts of the seas has been killed off by heavy pollution.

Birds
Dozens of seabird species, including albatrosses, cormorants, terns, pelicans, penguins, and many other birds, eat lots of fish. Without this source of food, they would starve.

Mammals

The many mammals that rely on fish to eat would probably become extinct. These include seals, dolphins, hunting whales, and otters.

What if fish were grown on farms?

Fish farming is carried out in many parts of the world. Trout, catfish, carp, and similar fish are grown in huge tanks or sealed lakes. They are fed and given clean, fresh water. Salmon and other saltwater fish are grown in huge wire-mesh cages suspended in the sea. They are also protected in these farms.

As a result, we have been able to provide a reliable source of fish. Before long we may be able to use fish farming to get all of our fish, without having to deplete natural fish stocks in the sea.

Disappearing fish stocks

Modern fishing is big business, with modern fishing boats, using sonar equipment to find schools of fish, and enormous nets to catch them in. Every day these fleets of trawlers take vast quantities of fish from the sea.

However, the size of the fish and the number of fish taken has been decreasing in many parts of the oceans. In some places, such as the Grand Banks off the coast of Canada, fish have virtually disappeared. The fish cannot breed quickly enough to replace the numbers that humans catch.

Invertebrates

Squid, octopuses, crabs, lobsters, jellyfish, anemones, and many other invertebrates (animals without backbones) hunt or catch a huge variety of fish to eat; or they might feed off their decaying bodies. Without fish, they may turn on each other for food.

FACTFILE

The ocean sunfish produces an astonishing 30 million eggs, each about 0.05 inches (1.3 mm) in diameter, every time it spawns.

In contrast, the mouth-brooding cichlid found in Lake Tanganyika, Africa, only produces seven eggs for reproduction.

The most expensive fish in the world is the Russian sturgeon. These fish are prized for their eggs, which are eaten as caviar. One sturgeon yielded nearly $300,000!

Piranha are said to be the most ferocious freshwater fish in the world. In 1981, following the capsize of a ferry in Brazil, nearly 300 people were reportedly killed by these blood-thirsty fish.

Some fish, known as brotulids, have been discovered at 27,230 feet (8,300 m) below sea level!

Electric eels from South America can produce electrical discharges that have been measured at 650 volts.

The largest fish in the world is the whale shark. The biggest seen was 56 feet (17 m) and weighed 30 to 35 tons.

The shortest fish is the Chagos dwarf goby, which is only 0.3 inches (8 mm) long.

The biggest shark ever caught with a rod and line was a great white shark that weighed over a ton!

Sailfish

Flying fish

Pike

Lungfish

Gar

Mackerel

Catfish

Dover sole

Bony fish 21,000 species

GLOSSARY

Biodiversity
The number of different species of plants and animals found in one area.

Bony fish
A fish whose skeleton is made from bone.

Cartilaginous fish
A fish whose skeleton is made from cartilage.

Diurnal
A fish that is awake during the day and asleep at night is called diurnal.

Fins
The parts of the body that the fish uses to control its movement through the water.

Gills
The feather-like organs, situated on either side of the head, just behind the eyes. These absorb oxygen from the water as it flows over them.

Lateral line
The silvery line that runs down the length of the fish on either side. It is extremely sensitive and detects any vibrations in the water.

Nocturnal
A fish that sleeps during the day and is awake at night is called nocturnal.

School
A group of fish that swim together. They can number up to several thousand. Also called a shoal.

Skeleton
The structure that supports the body of a living organism. A fish's skeleton can be made from either bone or cartilage.

Spawn
When fish reproduce, it is called spawning.

Swim bladder
The spongy organ inside all bony fish which helps them to regulate the depth at which they swim.

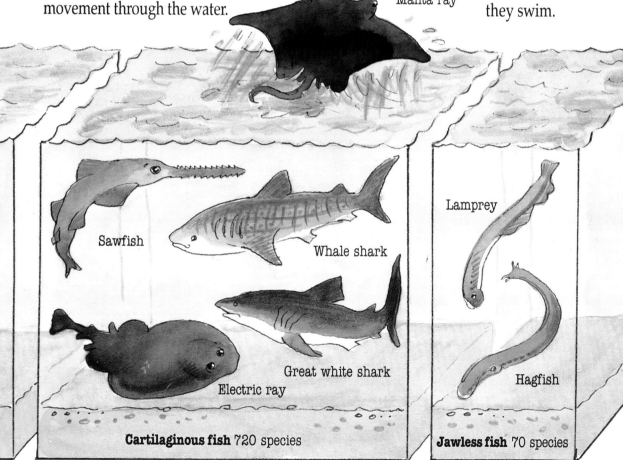

Manta ray

Sawfish

Whale shark

Great white shark

Electric ray

Cartilaginous fish 720 species

Lamprey

Hagfish

Jawless fish 70 species

INDEX

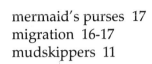